SUFFO LIFEBC

GW00360988

A portrait in photographs and old postcards

Nicholas Leach

John Nickalls Publications

By the same author
Lifeboats
For Those in Peril: The Lifeboat Service of the UK and Republic of Ireland
Cornwall's Lifeboat Heritage
The Waveney Lifeboats

First published in 2001 by John Nickalls Publications,
Oak Farm Bungalow, Suton, Wymondham, Norfolk. NR18 9SH

ISBN 1 904136 00 1

Printed by MFP Design and Print
Longford Trading Estate, Thomas Street, Stretford, Manchester M32 0JT

The author, Nicholas Leach has a long-standing interest in lifeboats and the history of the lifeboat service. He has visited every lifeboat station in Suffolk, past and present, and has written a number of books and articles on the subject including a comprehensive book containing details of every RNLI lifeboat station, which was published in 1999 to coincide with the Institution's 175th anniversary. He is currently Assistant Editor of *Ships Monthly* magazine.

Front cover upper: Launch of *Abdy Beauclerk* from Aldeburgh beach. (From an old postcard in the author's collection)

Front cover lower: Lowestoft lifeboat *Spirit of Lowestoft*. (Nicholas Leach)

Title page: 37ft 6in Rother *James Cable* approaching Aldeburgh beach. (From a postcard in the author's collection)

Back cover: Southwold Atlantic 75 lifeboat *Leslie Tranmer*. (Nicholas Leach)

Contents

The memorial in Aldeburgh churchyard to the seven men lost when the lifeboat *Aldeburgh* capsized on service in December 1899. The inscription reads: "In response to signals of distress, a crew of 18 brave men manned the lifeboat *Aldeburgh,* which was speedily launched in the teeth of an easterly gale and a heavy rolling sea. At duty's call to rescue others, with their own lives in their hands, these brave men went afloat, when alas! the boat capsizing seven of them met their end and lie buried here." (Nicholas Leach)

Historical introduction

This book tells the history of Suffolk's lifeboat stations and their lifeboats in postcards and photographs, old and new. The illustrations provide a detailed snapshot of the happenings and lifeboats at each station and show how the service in the county has developed. This introduction, necessarily brief, is intended as a background to the history of lifeboats and lifeboat work in Suffolk, whose lifeboat stations have impressive records for gallantry of which both crews and supporters are justly proud. Over the past two centuries, many lives have been saved by the lifeboat men and women of Suffolk, displaying considerable bravery and courage.

The Suffolk coast is characterised by long sandy beaches and crumbling cliffs. Much of the land is low-lying with erosion by the sea a constant threat. The shallow mudflats and dangerous sandbanks off the coastline have proved hazardous to generations of people using the sea. As these sandbanks and the channels are constantly changing, particularly in times of bad weather, navigation through them has always been both difficult and dangerous. The Newcombe Sands and Sizewell Bank close to the Suffolk shore represent a serious hazard to shipping, as do the Shipwash Sands at the southern end of the county, off Orfordness.

The first initiative to improve vessels' safety at sea helped them navigate past the most dangerous parts of the coast. During the 17th and 18th centuries, shipping lanes off Norfolk and Suffolk were improved by the placing of lights, usually in purpose-built lighthouses, to mark the major hazards. In Suffolk, lights were displayed at Lowestoft (the current tower was built in 1676 although it has been modernised several times since), Orfordness (1792) and Southwold (1890), and several others were built in Norfolk. While these helped vessels navigate the coastline, they were of no use once a vessel had foundered.

Despite obvious and considerable dangers faced by vessels passing the East Anglian coast, no lifeboats were provided in Suffolk until the 19th century. By the early years of the century sufficient money was available to fund lifeboats reflecting an increasing concern for the safety of vessels off Britain's coasts during the 1780s and 1790s. By 1800, steps had been taken to provide lifeboats, the first of which were designed and built by Henry Greathead at South Shields on the river Tyne. These 'Greathead' or 'North Country' type lifeboats were placed at strategic points so that if vessels did founder their crews and cargoes could be saved.

The earliest lifeboat in Suffolk was stationed at Lowestoft where, in 1800, a subscription had been raised to buy a lifeboat. It was built to Greathead's design and arrived at Lowestoft in 1801. However, the Greathead type of boat was not suitable for the seas off Lowestoft, having been built with the sea conditions on the north east coast in mind. The North Country type was not designed to be launched from an open beach, but was most suitable for work in shallow, broken surf close inshore. Therefore, the beachmen, who were expected to man it, were not impressed. In fact, they so disliked the boat that it was only used twice before being moved north to Gorleston.

The failure of the 1801 lifeboat reflected local prejudices against the Greathead design. However, as Lowestoft was an important port on the east coast trade route, the need for a lifeboat – to a design which would meet with the approval of the local beachmen – was considerable. Thus, under the supervision of Lionel Lukin, a London coachbuilder, a lifeboat was built similar in design to local beach yawls. The boat, named *Francis Ann,* was intended for local conditions, so gained the confidence of the local beachmen and was perated successfully for many years.

Francis Ann can be regarded as the first sailing lifeboat to be built, and the first of the 'Norfolk & Suffolk' type lifeboats. During the 19th century, this design was perfected and became the standard lifeboat type for the lifeboat stations of East Anglia. These were large boats, up to 46ft in length, which had almost flat bottoms ideally suited to working in the shallow waters encountered around the sandbanks. Because of their size, however, they were virtually unmanageable under oars and were thus intended primarily for sailing; they had a huge sail area, which consisted of a dipping fore lug and standing mizzen, enabling them to cover long distances.

At the same time as the first Lowestoft lifeboat was built, another Greathead boat was ordered for operation at Bawdsey Haven, some 40 miles to the south of Lowestoft. This boat arrived a month after the Lowestoft one, and seems to have been better used. In 1806, it came under the control of the Suffolk Humane Society, which had been formed at a meeting held in Kessingland in January 1806. This philanthropic organisation was also responsible for Francis Ann at Lowestoft, and retained control of both the Pakefield (which it established in 1840) and Lowestoft stations until 1855.

In the 1820s, further attempts were made to station lifeboats at other places in Suffolk. The Suffolk Association for Saving the Lives of Shipwrecked Seamen, a district association of the Royal National Institution for the Preservation of Life from Shipwreck (the original name of the Royal National Lifeboat Institution), was founded in October 1824.

This Association funded lifeboats at Orford, Woodbridge and Sizewell.

Before the building of lifeboats, groups of men in many coastal villages in East Anglia were ready to help vessels in distress using their own boats. In the 18th and 19th centuries, many inhabitants of the coastal villages and hamlets depended on the sea for their livelihood; some were employed in fishing, others in attending to the needs of shipping that filled the busy trade routes off this part of the coast, and most in a combination of the two. Part of the work involved in assisting shipping was the salvaging, for profit, of vessels that had gone aground or been stranded on the local sandbanks. Beachmen, as those men doing this kind of work were known, became renowned for both salvaging vessels stranded off the Norfolk and Suffolk coasts and saving lives from them.

The beachmen, organised into beach companies, owned and operated their own boats in which they would go to sea when a vessel was in difficulties. The ownership of the boat, a yawl, was usually divided equally between the members of the beach company. By helping casualties, they could often claim some kind of salvage award, the size of which could be quite sizeable compared to their usual relatively meagre income.

When purpose-built lifeboats began to be widely operated in Norfolk and Suffolk, the beachmen were the obvious candidates to man them. As they already had experience of life-saving in their own boats, they formed the lifeboat crew when a lifeboat was placed in their village. Although the beachmen maintained their own boats for salvage purposes, and also used these occasionally for

Aldeburgh No.2 lifeboat *Lucy Lavers* (ON.832) leaving Lowestoft harbour. It is not uncommon for lifeboats occasionally to leave their operational area, as on this occasion. *Lucy Lavers* was one of two motor lifeboats to serve at Aldeburgh during the 1940s and 1950s. (From an old photo supplied by a Shoreline member)

Lowestoft lifeboat
Spirit of Lowestoft,
a 47ft Tyne class, one
of the three modern
lifeboats now stationed
on the Suffolk coast.
(Peter Edey)

rescues, by the time the Royal National Lifeboat Institution (RNLI) had its lifeboats in place these were the primary means of rescuing vessels in difficulty.

Although the Suffolk Shipwreck Association was an offshoot of the RNLI, the national body did not operate Suffolk's lifeboat stations until the second half of the 19th century. In 1854, the Institution took over the station at Southwold where the independent local Lifeboat Society had operated the lifeboat for 14 years. The following year, the Institution took over the operations of the Suffolk Humane Society whose stations at Lowestoft, Pakefield, Thorpeness and Aldeburgh all came under the Institution's management. During the second half of the 19th century the RNLI expanded its operations. New stations were established at Corton in 1869 and Dunwich in 1873, while many of the existing stations were equipped with a No.2 lifeboat, smaller and lighter than the No.1 lifeboat, for inshore rescue work. By 1900, the expansion of lifeboat coverage meant that no fewer than ten lifeboats covered the Suffolk coast.

At this time, the internal combustion engine was being developed for marine purposes and in 1904 a lifeboat was fitted with an engine for the first time. Although there were many problems to be overcome to successfully operate an engine on board a lifeboat, once these had been solved lifeboats powered by the internal combustion engine could be operated with confidence. Initially, pulling and sailing lifeboats already in service were fitted with engines. However, further advances in design and development were delayed considerably due to the World War of

1914-18. Following the cessation of hostilities, the RNLI adopted a policy of modernisation which resulted in many new motor lifeboats being built to replace the pulling, sailing and steam lifeboats.

The first motor lifeboats in the East Anglian region arrived during the early 1920s. The first motor lifeboat in Suffolk was placed at Lowestoft in 1921 and another went to Southwold in 1925. The motorisation of the lifeboat fleet during the inter-war years, and the consequent improvement in coverage provided by the greater range of the motor lifeboats, reduced the need for so many stations. Therefore, many of the stations opened during the latter half of the 19th century were closed. Pakefield and Kessingland were closed in 1922 and 1936 respectively and by the outbreak of World War II the Suffolk coast was covered by only three motor lifeboats, operating from Lowestoft, Southwold and Aldeburgh.

In 1963, the RNLI introduced the inshore lifeboat in response to changing demands on the lifeboat service. As more people began using the sea for leisure during the 1960s, the number of inshore incidents to which lifeboats were called increased. The conventional lifeboats were not well suited to such work and it was clear that a simple, fast rescue craft was required for working inshore. In Suffolk, Southwold was one of the first eight stations to operate an inshore rescue boat. The 16ft inflatable lifeboats, made from tough nylon with neoprene, were crewed by two, powered by a 40hp outboard engine, and could be launched quickly and easily. The number of inshore rescue boats (later known as inshore lifeboats, abbreviated to ILBs) on station gradually increased. In 1977, an ILB was stationed at Aldeburgh to supplement the offshore lifeboat, and in 2001 an inland lifeboat station was established on a trial basis at Oulton Broad using a D class inflatable.

The lifeboats of Suffolk have been involved in many dramatic rescues. The most recent award-winning service shows that 21st century lifeboatmen, using the most sophisticated lifeboats yet built, are upholding the life-saving tradition of two centuries. The service began at 10.38am on 28 May 2000 when the Aldeburgh lifeboat, 12m Mersey *Freddie Cooper*, was launched under the command of Coxswain Ian Firman to go to the aid of the Netherlands registered yacht *Rose Bank* which was having difficulty steering in Force 9-10 severe gales and big seas.

After a difficult passage, during which the casualty's position was reported incorrectly on several occasions, the lifeboat finally reached the yacht at 11.56am having battled through six metre breaking seas. On reaching the casualty, Coxswain and crew were forced to contend with worsening conditions with seas, at times, up to 10 metres. Coxswain Firman opted to establish a tow but before it could be rigged, the skipper of the yacht decided that the safest option was to abandon ship because of the appalling sea conditions.

It was now 12.25pm and the lifeboat from Harwich, relief 17m Severn *Fraser Flyer (Civil Service No.43)*, had arrived so the two crews worked together to take off the yacht's crew. It was agreed that the transfer of the four crew, in itself a hazardous undertaking in the prevailing conditions, should be undertaken by the Aldeburgh lifeboat.

Two approaches made by the Aldeburgh lifeboat were aborted because of the yacht's pitching but contact was achieved on the third attempt. Once alongside, two men were hauled off the yacht but as this initial transfer was completed the lifeboat had to retreat due to the yacht's motion. During the fourth approach, the yacht's third crew member was so petrified that he initially refused to move. Coxswain Firman was forced to drive the lifeboat hard alongside, sustaining some damage, before the crew member felt safe enough to leave the yacht and board the lifeboat. The skipper got off on the fifth approach after which the lifeboat pulled clear of the yacht.

The Harwich lifeboat escorted the Mersey into calmer waters. Two of the survivors were seasick, all were traumatised and the lifeboat crew looked after them until they arrived on land. None of the lifeboat crew were injured and the lifeboat functioned well throughout. Although damage was sustained to the guard rails, fendering and paintwork, it was only superficial and did not affect the serviceability of the lifeboat.

The service, which had taken six hours, was described by Martyn Smith, divisional inspector for the East: "Coxswain Firman and his crew, two of whom were young and inexperienced, exhibited great fortitude and determination in what were appalling conditions. Throughout the service, the Coxswain exhibited firm leadership, clarity of thought and sound decision-making. He proved himself to be a capable seaman in that he successfully transferred four casualties in very poor conditions without injury to the lifeboat. It is unlikely the crew would have performed in the manner in which they did without the utmost faith and confidence in Coxswain Firman."

For this outstanding rescue, Coxswain/ Mechanic Firman was awarded the RNLI's Bronze Medal. Deputy Second Coxswain Lee Firman, Joint Assistant Mechanic Allan Warner, and crew members Jason Burns, Adrian Burns, John Andrews and Chris Spooner received Medal service certificates.

Acknowledgements

This book could not have been produced without the assistance of the following people, who kindly made their postcards and photographs available to me, and to whom I am extremely grateful: Jeff Morris, Coventry; Paul Russell, Hitchin; David Gooch, Houghton Regis; Roger Wiltshire, Norwich; Tony Denton, Shrewsbury; John Cragie; Stuart Jones and the Port of Lowestoft Research Society; Adrian Vicary, of the Maritime Photographic Library, Cromer; Peter Edey, Brightlingsea; W J Keith, Lowestoft; Gary Markham, Caister; and Gary Doy, Southwold.

Nicholas Leach, June 2001

Lowestoft

Frances Ann, 1807-49

In 1802, a lifeboat built by Henry Greathead at South Shields was purchased for use at Lowestoft. However, the beachmen refused to man it, preferring instead their own large, powerful sailing yawls. When the Suffolk Humane Society was formed in 1807, the committee agreed that a sailing lifeboat should be constructed on similar lines to those of the beachmen's yawls. Designed by Lionel Lukin, of London, constructed on the North Beach by Batchelor Barcham, and launched on 19 November 1807, *Frances Ann* was the first lifeboat of what became known as the 'Norfolk & Suffolk' type. Named after the counties in which the design originated, Norfolk & Suffolk type lifeboats were operated extensively throughout East Anglia. Although it was similar in build and rig to the yawls favoured by the beachmen, the new lifeboat had additional buoyancy as well as greater ballast for improved stability.

Samuel Plimsoll (ON.22), 1876-1905

Watched by a large crowd, the 44ft Norfolk & Suffolk lifeboat *Samuel Plimsoll* is launched off the North Beach at Lowestoft. This photograph gives an idea of how much physical effort was required to launch the large sailing lifeboats off the flat, exposed beaches of East Anglia. The lifeboat was named after Samuel Plimsoll, the MP for Derby, where funds for the boat were raised. Plimsoll campaigned to improve conditions in the Merchant Navy, named the lifeboat at a ceremony on 21 December 1876 on North Beach. (From an old postcard supplied by David Gooch)

Samuel Plimsoll (ON.22) at moorings in the harbour

Samuel Plimsoll at moorings in the harbour, close to the fishing smacks. During her first years on station this lifeboat was launched off the beach (see top picture), but as the harbour was gradually developed keeping her afloat became a viable option. In 1882, it was proposed that she should be kept afloat in the winter months, and a mooring was made available at the inner end of the North Pier, as shown in this photograph. (Roger Wiltshire)

Volunteer lifeboat *Carolina Hamilton*, 1883-93

The establishment of a volunteer lifeboat came about following the great gale of 28 October 1882 during which there was a delay in launching *Samuel Plimsoll,* blamed in part on the Coxswain, Bob Hook. *Carolina Hamilton,* a Norfolk & Suffolk lifeboat operated independently for ten years, was provided by the Great Eastern Railway Co and named after the chairman's wife. Hook became Coxswain of the independent boat after resigning as Coxswain of the RNLI lifeboats following the 1882 incident. (Port of Lowestoft Research Society)

The Pier Entrance and *Carolina Hamilton* lifeboat

Lowestoft harbour was developed during the first half of the 19th century. As the harbour grew and trade expanded, a railway line to the port was opened in 1859. This was taken over in 1862 by the Great Eastern Railway Co, who further developed the harbour. The lifeboat provided by the Company, the 48ft *Carolina Hamilton,* can be seen here passing the wooden lighthouse at the end of the South Pier. (From a postcard in the Gordon Campbell Collection, courtesy of Jeff Morris)

Stock Exchange (ON.288), 1890-92

Built at Lowestoft, the 46ft Norfolk & Suffolk lifeboat *Stock Exchange,* funded by the Stock Exchange, was stationed at Lowestoft in June 1890. She was used in the lifeboat trails in early 1892 but, during these, was damaged so badly that the beachmen refused to man her, so was removed having been on station for less than two years. (Port of Lowestoft Research Society)

Lifeboat Trials, April 1892

During the early 1890s, the RNLI organised trials of various lifeboat types to assess and compare them in different conditions. Trials were held at Lowestoft in 1892 and Montrose in 1893. At Lowestoft, four lifeboats participated: a 44ft self-righter; a 43ft Watson sailing lifeboat; a 43ft Tubular lifeboat; and the Lowestoft lifeboat *Stock Exchange* (ON.288), a 46ft 6in Norfolk & Suffolk. The trials were concluded on 19 April 1892 and the Watson lifeboat was deemed best by the coxswains who took the boats to sea. In this photograph, the large 44ft self-righter, *Thomas Simcox* (ON.312) from the Dungeness station, can be seen nearest the camera being prepared for launching. (Port of Lowestoft Research Society)

Stock Exchange (ON.356), 1893-1912

After the beachmen had rejected the first *Stock Exchange* (ON.288), a new lifeboat was built for the station incorporating the improvements suggested during the lifeboat trials, such as water ballast tanks. This second *Stock Exchange* (ON.356), completed in 1893, arrived in July and served as the No.2 lifeboat until 1912. A 46ft Norfolk & Suffolk type, like her predecessor she was funded by the Stock Exchange Lifeboat Fund. (Port of Lowestoft Research Society)

Kentwell (ON.543), 1905-21

The 46ft Norfolk & Suffolk type *Kentwell* under sail off Lowestoft harbour. As the No.1 lifeboat from 1905 until 1921, she is credited with saving 168 lives in 60 service launches. On 22 November 1914 she was involved in the rescue of crews from two minesweepers for which her Coxswain, John Swan, was awarded the Silver medal. The first minesweeper, HMS *Spider,* had been driven onto a beach near Lowestoft, and from her 13 men were saved by the lifeboat. Later on the same day, HMS *Condor* ran aground on the Newcombe Sands in heavy breaking seas, and *Kentwell* was used to save her crew of nine. (From an old print supplied by W J Keith)

Kentwell (ON.543), 1905-21

Since 1882 the lifeboat had been kept afloat in the harbour, an unusual practice in the 19th and early 20th centuries. However, because the lifeboats favoured in East Anglia were large, thus difficult to manhandle on a beach, keeping the boat afloat was a practical idea. In this photograph, *Kentwell* can be seen moored alongside a raft of small fishing boats at the port's Fish Market. At 46ft in length, this lifeboat was one of the largest sailing lifeboats ever built. (From an old postcard supplied by David Gooch)

Reserve Lifeboat _Hugh Taylor_ (ON.629)

Built in 1912, the 36ft Norfolk & Suffolk type *Hugh Taylor* spent ten years at stations in East Anglia before being placed in the RNLI's Reserve Fleet. This photograph, probably dating from the 1920s, shows her outside the lifeboat houses at Lowestoft on her launching carriage. Two lifeboat houses were built on the North Beach for the station's two lifeboats, but both were demolished in the 1970s. (Photograph from the Jeff Morris Collection)

Norfolk & Suffolk motor lifeboat *Agnes Cross* (ON.663), 1921-39

In 1921, the new motor lifeboat for Gorleston, *John and Mary Meiklam of Gladswood*, was completed at the Cowes yard of S E Saunders. She went on station in February 1921 but, following crewing difficulties, was transferred to Lowestoft on 31 March. She was renamed *Agnes Cross* after being appropriated to the gift of Mrs Agnes Cross, South Kensington, London. This photograph shows her at her moorings at the inner end of the North Pier in 1925. (MPL)

Coxswain John Swan and *Agnes Cross* (ON.663)

An early photograph of *Agnes Cross*, Lowestoft's first motor lifeboat, with Coxswain John Swan and his crew on board. Swan, appointed Coxswain in 1911, was awarded the Gold medal for the rescue of the steamship *Hopelyn* in the early hours of 21 October 1922. The rescue involved taking *Agnes Cross* alongside the casualty, which was wrecked on the North Scroby Sands, to save 24 men and a black kitten in gale force winds. The Silver medal was awarded to Mechanic Ralph Scott and Bronze medals to the crew. (From an old print supplied by W J Keith)

***Agnes Cross* (ON.663), 1921-39**

Agnes Cross, a 46ft 6in Norfolk & Suffolk motor lifeboat, was stationed at Lowestoft from 1921 to 1939 during which time she launched 124 times and saved 209 lives. She was the first motor lifeboat to be stationed at Lowestoft, and one of the RNLI's earliest purpose-built motor lifeboats. Like all early motor lifeboats, she was fitted with one engine, as opposed to two, a 60hp 4-cylinder Tylor unit giving a top speed of 8.3 knots. After being replaced at Lowestoft in 1939, she was placed in the Reserve Fleet. (Port of Lowestoft Research Society)

Michael Stephens (ON.838), 1939-63

The 46ft Watson cabin motor *Michael Stephens,* on station between October 1939 and 1963, leaving harbour. While stationed at Lowestoft, she saved 73 lives and launched 134 times, including many wartime services. She was one of the lifeboats that helped with the Dunkirk evacuation in the summer of 1940, assisting the Southwold and Walmer lifeboats. After service at Lowestoft, she went to Exmouth and was then used as a Relief lifeboat until being sold out of service in 1976, more than 35 years after being built. (Port of Lowestoft Research Society)

Michael Stephens (ON.838), 1961

Michael Stephens moored alongside the jetty at the seaward side of Hamilton Dock in August 1961. She had a shallower draft than the standard 46ft Watson so she could operate with greater ease near the shallow sandbanks encountered off the Suffolk coast. The moorings at Hamilton Dock were used until February 1969, when new moorings found. (Jeff Morris)

Coxswain Harry Burgess and crew on board *Michael Stephens* (ON.838)

Harry Burgess was appointed Coxswain in April 1953 following the sudden death of Coxswain Albert Spurgeon. Burgess had seen service with the Royal Navy but was released for lifeboat work at the special request of the RNLI. In this photograph he is seen with the lifeboat crew on board 46ft Watson *Michael Stephens*. One of the most notable rescues in which he was involved took place on 24 February 1961 when, throughout the night, *Michael Stephens* stood by the motor vessel *Gudveig*, aground on the Cross Sands. At daybreak both vessels were covered with snow and ice. The lifeboatmen suffered greatly from cold and exposure, so much so that Burgess was ill for a fortnight afterwards. He retired from service in 1969 having served in the lifeboat crew for 36 years. (From an old photo supplied by W J Keith)

Frederick Edward Crick (ON.970), 1963-86

The 47ft Watson cabin motor lifeboat *Frederick Edward Crick* was placed on station at Lowestoft in July 1963. She was funded from the legacy of Mrs Florence May Crick, of Longfield, Kent. This photograph shows her in August 1964 in Hamilton Dock at moorings which were used until February 1969. The jetty, visible towards the boat's stern, was demolished shortly afterwards. (Jeff Morris)

Frederick Edward Crick (ON.970) on exercise

Frederick Edward Crick on exercise with an air-sea rescue helicopter off the South Pier. Since World War II helicopters have been used increasingly for search and rescue operations and this photograph shows cooperation between the rescue services during the 1960s. During her operational life at Lowestoft, *Frederick Edward Crick* was launched on service 247 times, and saved 109 lives. (From an old postcard supplied by David Gooch)

Frederick Edward Crick (ON.970), 1963-86

The 47ft Watson cabin motor lifeboat *Frederick Edward Crick* at moorings in the Yacht Basin. The wooden boarding boat, seen moored to the left, was used by the crew to reach the lifeboat. This photograph of the Yacht Basin was taken from the South Pier, with the lifeboat the most prominent vessel in the harbour. (From a postcard supplied by David Gooch)

Lowestoft lifeboat crew

The lifeboat crew on board *Frederick Edward Crick* in the late 1960s: Coxswain Harry Burgess (in cap) standing between Honorary Secretary Michael Chapman to the right, and Mrs Irene Craig. The other crew are, from left to right, Peter Gibbons, Billy Thorpe, Billy Keith, Jack Rose, Jack Stoddart and Harold Robinson. (From an old photo supplied by W J Keith)

Reserve Lifeboat *Canadian Pacific* (ON.803), 1974

During 1974 when *Frederick Edward Crick* went for overhaul, she was replaced temporarily by *Canadian Pacific,* one of the RNLI's reserve lifeboats. Built in 1938 and stationed at Selsey until 1969, *Canadian Pacific* served as a reserve lifeboat until 1977. In this photograph, the deck layout is clearly shown. Pre-1939 46ft Watson lifeboats, such as *Canadian Pacific,* were built with open aft cockpits which were later enclosed. (P A Vicary, courtesy of Paul Russell)

Rescue by *Frederick Edward Crick* (ON.970), 1978

Frederick Edward Crick towing the 44-ton gaff cutter *Jolie Brise* into harbour on 30 August 1978. The cutter, built in 1913, was taking part in the Tall Ships race on her way from Oslo to Harwich when she developed engine problems. (Eastern Daily Press, by courtesy of Paul Russell)

Naming ceremony of Gorleston lifeboat *Barham* (ON.1065), 1980

On 17 September 1980 the Lowestoft lifeboat *Frederick Edward Crick* paid a courtesy visit to the neighbouring station of Gorleston to attend the naming ceremony of 44ft Waveney *Barham*. The two lifeboats are seen here together off the harbour entrance. (Jeff Morris)

Frederick Edward Crick (ON.970), 1983

47ft Watson *Frederick Edward Crick* at moorings in the Yacht Basin in August 1983. These moorings were used from 1972 to 1998, with crew facilities on the adjacent quayside in the premises of the Royal Norfolk & Suffolk Yacht Club. On the after end of the boat's substructure can be seen the cylindrical casing in which the self-righting air-bag was housed. This gave the boat a once-only self-righting capability. In the background can be seen the South Pier Pavilion which was later demolished to make way for a new lifeboat crew facility. (Nicholas Leach)

City of London (ON.1074)

During the early 1980s, the RNLI developed the 47ft Tyne, a new fast lifeboat for stations where slipway launching was employed. The prototype *City of London*, allocated to Selsey, visited Lowestoft on 2 September 1982 prior to her naming ceremony in London. Because of the Tyne's steel hull and protected propellers, she was ideal for stations such as Lowestoft where the lifeboat might have to take the ground during rescues. Behind *City of London*, relief lifeboat *T. G. B.* (ON.962) is on relief duty. (Lowestoft Journal, courtesy of Paul Russell)

Relief Lifeboats, 1986

In February 1986, *Frederick Edward Crick* was replaced by a 47ft Tyne, but before the new lifeboat was ready, temporary lifeboats were stationed at Lowestoft. Relief 46ft 9in Watson *Charles Henry Ashley* (ON.866), on the right, took over temporarily from *Frederick Edward Crick*, and in October 1986 was herself replaced by relief 52ft Barnett *Archibald and Alexander M Paterson* (ON.924), on the left. This photograph shows the two boats in the Yacht Basin on 19 October 1986. (Paul Russell)

52ft Barnett *Archibald and Alexander M Paterson* (ON.924), 1986

Built in 1955 for Stromness, 52ft Barnett *Archibald and Alexander M Paterson* was placed on station at Lowestoft as a temporary measure prior to the arrival of the station's new 47ft Tyne. Seen here in the Yacht Basin on 22 October 1986, three days after going on station, she served for just over a year during which time she launched 18 times on service. (Tony Denton)

Arrival of *Spirit of Lowestoft* (ON.1132), 1987

52ft Barnett *Archibald and Alexander M Paterson* leading in the new 47ft Tyne *Spirit of Lowestoft* on 9 November 1987. This was a notable day for the station and a proud day for the town. The new boat, funded through the efforts of local people and local appeals, was the first new lifeboat at the port for almost a quarter of a century. (Jeff Morris)

Naming Ceremony of *Spirit of Lowestoft* (ON.1132), 1988

Before the naming ceremony of 47ft Tyne *Spirit of Lowestoft,* no fewer than three lifeboats were moored in the Yacht Basin. Background left is Gorleston's 44ft Waveney *Barham* (ON.1065), on a courtesy visit for the ceremony, while background right can be seen relief 47ft Tyne *Good Shepherd* (ON.1115) at the usual lifeboat moorings standing in for *Spirit of Lowestoft,* moored in the foreground, during the ceremony. (Paul Russell)

Naming Ceremony of *Spirit of Lowestoft* (ON.1132), 1988

The scene in the Trawl Dock during the naming and dedication ceremony of Lowestoft's new 47ft Tyne *Spirit of Lowestoft* took place on 26 May 1988. Funded through the Lowestoft Lifeboat Appeal, which raised some £450,000, the new lifeboat was dedicated by the Rector of Lowestoft, Canon Paul Alton, and christened by HRH The Duke of Kent. In attendance at the ceremony, seen to the right, was 44ft Waveney *Barham* (ON.1065) from Gorleston. (Jeff Morris)

Arbroath lifeboat *Inchcape* (ON.1194) on passage, 1993

When new lifeboats are completed, they are taken to the RNLI's Depot at Poole in Dorset, where their crews train on them and then take them to their new station. Lifeboats on passage along the east coast often call at Lowestoft for refuelling and here, 12m Mersey *Inchcape*, destined for Arbroath, is visiting on 2 May 1993 while travelling to her station in Scotland. The station's own lifeboat, *Spirit of Lowestoft,* is at moorings in the Yacht Basin. (Paul Russell)

Relief Lifeboat *Sam and Joan Woods* (ON.1075), 1996

The second 47ft Tyne to be built, *Sam and Joan Woods,* served in the Relief Fleet after her evaluation trials. She was on temporary duty at Lowestoft a number of times, and is seen here in the Yacht Basin during a relief duty between 18 May and 6 July 1996. (W J Keith)

Relief Lifeboat *John Fison* (ON.1060), 1998

During 1998, 44ft Waveney *John Fison* served as a relief lifeboat in place of the station's 47ft Tyne which was being re-engined. *John Fison* was originally stationed at Harwich, and then served as a relief lifeboat. It was unusual for a 44ft Waveney to operate from Lowestoft, but she was well liked at the station. (Nicholas Leach)

New shore facility, 1998

As part of the RNLI's policy of upgrading shore facilities in the 1990s, a new shore facility was built in the south-eastern corner of the Yacht Basin in 1998, on the site of the old pavilion which had been demolished. The new building provided greatly improved crew facilities, including changing and drying rooms, a workshop, crew training room and fuel storage. A new pontoon berth for the lifeboat was located nearby in the redeveloped Yacht Basin. (Gary Markham)

Netherlands lifeboat *Dorus Rijkers* at Lowestoft, 1999

On several occasions, lifeboats from the Netherlands have crossed to East Anglia for courtesy visits to RNLI lifeboat stations. Here, 14.4m rigid-inflatable *Dorus Rijkers,* built in 1997, stationed at Den Helder and operated by the KNRM (Royal Dutch Lifeboat Society), is refuelled alongside *Spirit of Lowestoft* on 6 March 1999. (Gary Markham)

Retirement of Coxswain John Catchpole, 2000

In May 2000 John Catchpole retired as Coxswain of the Lowestoft lifeboat after 27 years of service. He became Coxswain in 1984 and was twice awarded the Bronze medal for outstanding rescues. This photograph shows Coxswain Catchpole (back, fourth from right) with the lifeboat crew on board *Spirit of Lowestoft* on 16 April 2000. (Peter Edey)

Spirit of Lowestoft (ON.1132), 1988 to date

47ft Tyne *Spirit of Lowestoft* passing the harbour on 28 May 2000 during her routine Sunday morning exercise, the last undertaken with John Catchpole as Coxswain. (Peter Edey)

Gorleston lifeboat *Samarbeta* (ON.1208) at Lowestoft

Lowestoft's closest neighbouring lifeboat station is that at Great Yarmouth & Gorleston, and for the retirement of John Catchpole as Coxswain, 14m Trent *Samarbeta* from Gorleston visited Lowestoft. She is seen here moored alongside Lowestoft's own lifeboat, 47ft Tyne *Spirit of Lowestoft,* in the south-eastern corner of the Yacht Basin. (Peter Edey)

Memorial Plaque to *Samuel Plimsoll*

One of several plaques mounted on the railings around the Yacht Club depicts the lifeboat *Samuel Plimsoll* (ON.22). This lifeboat served the station from 1876 until 1922 and is credited with saving 165 lives. (Nicholas Leach)

Lifeboat Memorial, 2000

In 2000, an impressive 14ft high statue was erected on the south side of the river Waveney beside the bascule bridge as a memorial to all lifeboatmen. The statue, commissioned by Lowestoft Lifeboatmen's Sports and Social Club, was officially unveiled by MP Bob Blizzard on Saturday 24 June 2000 as a millennium memorial to all the port's lifeboatmen, past, present and future. It was created by sculptor Dominic Marshall out of cold-cast bronze and cost £13,000. A commemorative plaque on the base dedicates it to lifeboatmen "for their sterling duty to seafarers of the world." (Nicholas Leach)

Pakefield

Two Sisters, Mary and Hannah (ON.23), 1872-1910

Built in 1872, *Two Sisters, Mary and Hannah* served at Pakefield as the No.1 lifeboat. A large 46ft 3in Norfolk & Suffolk type, she was originally named *Sisters* but was renamed in 1876 after being appropriated to the gift of the late Thomas Perkin, of Wigton. She was moved from Pakefield in 1886 after the proprietor of the site on which the lifeboat house was built took the land back. As a result, the No.1 station was closed leaving the smaller No.2 lifeboat to serve the area while *Two Sisters, Mary and Hannah* was taken to Lowestoft and stored. The station was re-established in 1890 following the acquisition of a new site and the building of a new boathouse. *Two Sisters, Mary and Hannah* returned from Lowestoft, where she had been used to save 90 lives, and remained on station until August 1910. (From an old postcard supplied by David Gooch)

Two Sisters, Mary and Hannah (ON.23)

Built in 1872 as _Sisters_ but subsequently, renamed _Two Sisters, Mary and Hannah_ served as the No.1 lifeboat until 1910 during which time she saved 145 lives. This photograph shows the elegant lines of the Norfolk & Suffolk design. The large dipping fore lug and standing mizzen enabled a huge spread of canvas to be raised, but a high standard of seamanship was needed to handle the craft, particularly in storm conditions and strong winds. Two large drop keels were fitted to provide the leverage needed to utilise the power of the extensive sail area. (Port of Lowestoft Research Society)

James Leath (ON.607), 1910-19

In August 1910 a new 42ft Norfolk & Suffolk type lifeboat was placed on station at Pakefield, replacing _Two Sisters, Mary and Hannah_ (ON.23). The new lifeboat, named _James Leath_ after the donor whose legacy funded the boat, later served at Caister and Aldeburgh before being sold out of service in 1935. In this photograph, she is being hauled across the beach prior to launching. (From an old photo supplied by a Shoreline member)

James Leath (ON.607), 1910-19

James Leath being hauled across the beach over skids, watched by a large crowd on what was probably the station's annual lifeboat day. *James Leath* was one of more than 100 lifeboats built by the Thames Iron Works at Blackwall during the late 19th and early 20th centuries. Weighing well over 8 tons, considerable effort was required to move the lifeboat across the sand, hence the large number of helpers. (Port of Lowestoft Research Society)

Launching *James Leath* (ON.607)

This fine view of *James Leath* shows her setting out from the beach at Pakefield. She was the last large lifeboat to serve at Pakefield, being replaced in November 1919 by a smaller 34ft Norfolk & Suffolk type. She saved two lives while at Pakefield and was later stationed at Caister and Aldeburgh before being sold out of service in August 1935. She is now part of the Lifeboat Collection at Chatham Historic Dockyard. (From an old postcard supplied by David Gooch)

Hugh Taylor (ON.629), 1919-22

The much travelled 36ft Norfolk & Suffolk lifeboat *Hugh Taylor* was built in 1912 by Thames Iron Works for Great Yarmouth, where she served for seven years. She was transferred to Pakefield, later became a Reserve lifeboat, then went to Aldeburgh and finally Kessingland before being sold out of service in 1936. Although this photograph probably shows her at Great Yarmouth on the day of her inauguration ceremony, it is included with Pakefield because she was the last lifeboat to operate from this station before it was closed in 1922 after the motor lifeboat had been sent to Lowestoft. (From an old photo supplied by a Shoreline member)

No.2 Lifeboat House

Between 1871 and 1895 a second lifeboat was operated at Pakefield. A wooden lifeboat house was built on the beach in 1870, but after encroachment by the sea it was moved in 1887 to the site shown here. The house was sited beneath the cliffs and opposite the Grand Hotel, the building to the left. The No.2 station, as it was known, operated the 30ft *Henry Burford RN,* which was carriage launched. This lifeboat served throughout the life of the No.2 station, and is credited with saving 11 lives during 24 years on station. (Port of Lowestoft Research Society)

Kessingland

Bolton (ON.25) on the beach

The RNLI first provided a lifeboat at Kessingland in 1867. Three years later, a second lifeboat was sent to the station and stationed at Kessingland Beach. Named _Bolton_, she is seen here probably on the day of her formal inauguration in November 1870. A large 42ft 5in Norfolk & Suffolk lifeboat, she was provided by the people of Bolton who had spent months collecting money in their town. As well as funding the lifeboat house, visible to the left, the Bolton Lifeboat Fund also provided for the station's annual upkeep, a practice common in the late 19th century. This lifeboat was replaced in 1893 by the second _Bolton_ (ON.352), having saved 49 lives. (Port of Lowestoft Research Society)

Bolton (ON.352), 1893-1918

The second lifeboat to be funded by the Bolton Lifeboat Fund was sent to Kessingland in 1893 to replace the original *Bolton*. At a ceremony on 19 August 1893 this second *Bolton* lifeboat was named by the Mayor of Bolton, Alderman William Nicholson, who was also Chairman of the RNLI's Bolton Branch. The new lifeboat was a large Norfolk & Suffolk type, 43ft in length, built by Chambers & Colby at Lowestoft. (Port of Lowestoft Research Society)

Rehousing *Bolton* (ON.352), 1893-1918

The large 43ft Norfolk & Suffolk lifeboat *Bolton,* the second so named to serve at the station, being recovered and hauled into the lifeboat house. She served as the No.1 lifeboat until 1918, after which she was transferred to Southwold and sold in 1926. Unusually, in 1902 she was stationed temporarily at Aldeburgh while that station awaited its new lifeboat following the lifeboat disaster of 1899. In this photograph, the lifeboat is being hauled up the beach with her crew and the local Coastguard in attendance. (From an old postcard supplied by David Gooch)

St Paul (ON.406), 1897-1931

St Paul, a 38ft Norfolk & Suffolk type, launching from the beach at Kessingland, with a pushing pole being used by the shore helpers to get the boat through the surf. *St Paul* served as the No.2 lifeboat between 1897 and 1918, during which time she saved three lives. From 1918 until being replaced in 1931 she saved a further 15 lives after the large No.1 lifeboat *Bolton* (ON.352) had been withdrawn. She was one of many Norfolk & Suffolk type lifeboats built by the Great Yarmouth builder James Beeching. (From an old postcard supplied by a Shoreline member)

St Paul (ON.406), 1897-1931

Although the Norfolk & Suffolk lifeboat *St Paul* was only 38ft in length, and thus relatively light, a large number of helpers were needed to haul her from the lifeboat house. She was launched over skids laid on the beach. This boathouse is probably that built in the village in 1884, used for both No.1 and No.2 lifeboats. (Roger Wiltshire)

Launching No.2 lifeboat *St Paul* (ON.406)

This fine photograph of 38ft Norfolk & Suffolk *St Paul* clearly shows the clinker-built hull. The crew are wearing kapok life-jackets, introduced in 1904, but rather unpopular with crews because of their bulk. The masts are folded and, although the pushing pole can be seen on the boat's stern, there seems little hurry to get her afloat so this was almost certainly an exercise launch. (From an old postcard supplied by Roger Wiltshire)

Hugh Taylor (ON.629), 1931-36

The 36ft Norfolk & Suffolk lifeboat *Hugh Taylor* was the last lifeboat to serve at Kessingland, and when she was withdrawn in 1936 the station closed. She was built in 1912 and served at Great Yarmouth, Pakefield and Aldeburgh before coming to Kessingland. This photograph shows the boat being recovered on the beach. The heavy cork belting which can be seen around the gunwales was typical of the Norfolk & Suffolk design. (From an old photo supplied by a Shoreline member)

Southwold

Lifeboat crew, 1998

Southwld lifeboat crew and station officials with the station's second Atlantic 21, *The Quiver* (B-562), outside the inshore lifeboat house in September 1998. (Photo supplied by Gary Doy)

Harriett (ON.28), 1855-93

One of the first Southwold lifeboats was *Harriett,* a 40ft Norfolk & Suffolk built in 1855. This 19th century illustration shows her launching on service to the schooner *Princess Alice,* of Ipswich, on 28 January 1862. She had an eventful career at Southwold, remaining in service despite capsizing in February 1858 when three of those on board were lost. Alterations were made to her as a result of the accident, and in 1869 she was renamed *London Coal Exchange* after £700 had been donated by the Coal Merchants of London. During her time at Southwold she is credited with saving 67 lives. The lifeboat house pictured, under the North Cliff opposite where the lighthouse now stands, was completely undermined by the sea soon after this service.

Alfred Corry (ON.353), 1893-1918

Built in 1893, the 44ft Norfolk & Suffolk lifeboat *Alfred Corry* served at the No.1 station until 1918, during which time she saved 47 lives. Rigged with a dipping lug foresail and standing lug mizzen, she was also provided with 14 oars. She usually operated with a crew of 17 or 18 men, and was of the improved Norfolk & Suffolk type, taking on water ballast of approximately 5 tons. Funded from the legacy of Mr A J Corry, of Putney, she was named by Mrs J E Grubbe, wife of the Chairman of the Southwold Lifeboat Committee, on 3 April 1893. This photo shows her being launched with her mizzen sail raised. (From an old photo supplied by David Gooch)

Coxswain Sam May

This posed photograph depicts Southwold's famous coxswain Samuel Charles May wearing his cork life-jacket, with a rescue line at the ready. May was Coxswain from 1898 until 1918, during which time he received awards from two European governments. On 27 November 1905, he was in charge of the lifeboat which saved five from the fishing smack *Joseph et Yvonne,* of Dunkirk, for which he received a French Government silver medal. Bronze medals were awarded to the rest of the crew. He was presented with a silver medal by the Netherlands Government for the rescue of the Groningen schooner *Voorwarts'* crew of five on 17 January 1912. (From an old postcard supplied by Roger Wiltshire)

Rescue (ON.405), 1897-1920

In 1897 a new lifeboat was placed at the No.2 station. Built by Reynolds of Lowestoft and funded from the legacy of Mr J B Barkworth, brother of a former member of the local committee, the new lifeboat was a 32ft Norfolk & Suffolk type. She was exhibited at the Jubilee Exhibition in London in 1897 before going on station and was christened *Rescue* on 7 September 1897 by Mrs Barkworth. This photo was probably taken on the day of her naming. It shows the lifeboat being launched from the beach by carriage, unusual in Suffolk, but no doubt possible because of the boat's small size and weight. (From an old photo supplied by a Shoreline member)

Lifeboat Day 1908

The No.2 lifeboat *Rescue* (ON.405) served the station until 1920. Because she was launched from a carriage and at less than 4 tons was relatively light, it was possible to use her for fund-raising purposes. This photograph shows her being taken through Southwold in 1908 during the town's annual Lifeboat Day. (From an old postcard supplied by Roger Wiltshire)

Demonstration launch by *Rescue* (ON.405), 1908

Demonstration launch of No.2 lifeboat *Rescue* in 1908 as part of the town's annual Lifeboat Day. As the second lifeboat, *Rescue* was used for work inshore, with the larger sailing lifeboat going to vessels on the outlying sandbanks. During her 23 years at Southwold, *Rescue* was launched eight times on service and saved 20 lives. (From an old postcard supplied by Roger Wiltshire)

Recovery of *Rescue* (ON.405), 1908

Recovery of the No.2 lifeboat *Rescue* in 1908 during the town's annual Lifeboat Day. The lifeboat houses were built on the South Denes and the lifeboats were launched and recovered across the adjacent beach. The many spectators are dressed in their 'Sunday best' to watch the demonstration launch. (From an old postcard supplied by Roger Wiltshire)

Bolton (ON.352), 1918-25

The 43ft Norfolk & Suffolk lifeboat *Bolton* was built in 1893 for Kessingland, where she served at the No.1 station until October 1918. She was then transferred to the No.1 station at Southwold where she served until June 1925 and saved six lives. This photograph shows her moored in the river Blyth. (RNLI, courtesy of Jeff Morris)

Mary Scott (ON.691), 1925-40

The 46ft 6in motorised Norfolk & Suffolk lifeboat *Mary Scott,* on station from 1925 to 1940, was the first and last motor lifeboat to serve at Southwold. She is seen at her usual moorings in Southwold's small harbour, which was formed by the estuary of the river Blyth. Although the Norfolk & Suffolk sailing lifeboat was used extensively on the East Anglian coast, only three of the type were built with engines when motor lifeboats were introduced extensively into the lifeboat fleet during the inter-war years. (From an old postcard supplied by a Shoreline member)

Motor lifeboat *Mary Scott* (ON.691)

Mary Scott was on station for 15 years until the closure of Southwold harbour in 1940. Her most notable rescue during that time took place in 1927 when she stood by the Rotterdam steamship *Georgia* on 21 and 22 November. Although the steamship was on the Haisborough Sands, off Norfolk and some way out of Southwold lifeboat's area of operation, *Mary Scott* was called to assist after the Lowestoft lifeboat had been damaged. Coxswain Frank Upcraft was awarded the RNLI's Bronze medal for this service. (From an old postcard supplied by a Shoreline member)

Rescue by *Mary Scott* (ON.691), 1932

On 18 July 1932, *Mary Scott* was launched to the yacht *Damaris,* of Lowestoft. She saved the yacht and it two occupants and is seen in this photo towing the yacht into Southwold harbour. During 15 years on station, *Mary Scott* saved 23 lives. She was removed in 1940 because the harbour was closed by a boom placed across it as a wartime anti-invasion measure. (From an old postcard supplied by Paul Russell)

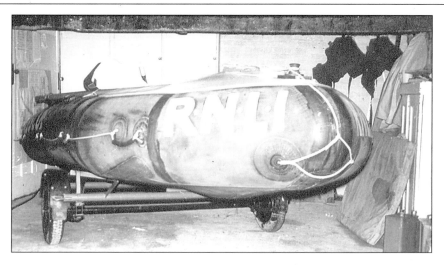

Inshore Lifeboat No.6, 1963

As more people began using the sea for leisure, so the type of casualties to which lifeboats were called changed. In 1962, in response to this change, the RNLI bought an inflatable boat for trials a a simple, fast rescue craft intended for working in moderate conditions. After trials, eight inshore rescue boats were introduced during 1963, one of which went to Southwold. This new craft, IRB No.6, seen here on 24 September 1963, was launched from a trolley and kept in an old storeroom a the far end of the harbour. (Jeff Morris)

Inshore Lifeboat No.36, 1966

The inshore lifeboats were 16ft inflatable lifeboats, made from tough nylon with neoprene, crewed by two or three, and powered by a 40hp outboard engine. They could be launched quickly and easily and this, coupled to their speed of 20 knots, meant their speed into and through the water was considerably faster than any lifeboat in service at the time of their introduction. IRB No.36, seen here on 20 September 1966, was another of the early inflatables. It served at Southwold from 1963 to 1970, cost £750 and saved 30 lives in service 69 launches. (Jeff Morris)

Inshore Lifeboat D-191, 1972

The success of the inshore rescue boats, later known as inshore lifeboats (ILBs), led to more and more places operating the boats during the 1960s. Many stations which had been established during the 19th century but were closed in the early 20th century were reopened to operate an ILB. Southwold was reopened and operated several ILBs. RFD PB16 type D-191, seen in September 1972, was on station from 1970 to 1973 and launched 75 times, saving 16 lives. (Jeff Morris)

Atlantic 21 *Solebay* (B-518), 1980

In July 1973, following trials the previous year, Atlantic 21 rigid-inflatable B-518 was placed on station at Southwold. Named *Solebay* after the first Southwold lifeboat, she served until 1985, launched 231 times on service and saved 92 lives. She is seen here speeding out of the harbour on service on 5 February 1980, but on this occasion the call proved to be a false alarm. The Atlantic, based on a design developed at the Atlantic College in Wales, had greater range, speed and capabilities than the standard ILB. (Eastern Daily Press, by courtesy of Paul Russell)

Launching Atlantic 21 *Solebay* (B-518), 1982

Atlantic 21 *Solebay* launching into the river Blyth on 19 September 1982. At the helm is Roger Trigg who was awarded the Bronze medal for a service performed on 16 January 1981 to the motor fishing vessel *Concord*. The fishing vessel, which had broken down east of Southwold Harbour in gale force winds, was towed by another fishing vessel to Lowestoft escorted by the Atlantic 21. The tow parted four times but on each occasion the ILB helped re-establish it, ensuring both boats safely reached harbour. (Jeff Morris)

ILB house at Blackshore

The inshore lifeboat station at Southwold, established in 1963, was one of the first ILB stations opened by the RNLI. In 1966 this purpose-built wooden ILB house was constructed at Blackshore, on the south bank of the river Blyth. Launching involved lowering the ILB stern first down the wooden ramp Atlantic 21 *Solebay* (B-518) can be seen in the house. (Nicholas Leach)

The Quiver (B-562), 1985-98

The second Atlantic 21 to serve at Southwold, *The Quiver* (B-562), entering the harbour at speed. Named after the 19th century lifeboats that were funded by the Quiver Magazine, she arrived on station in January 1985 and served until 1998. She was provided out of the legacy of Mrs D Q Presland and cost £29,000. (Eastern Daily Press, by courtesy of Paul Russell)

The Quiver (B-562), 1985-98

Atlantic 21 *The Quiver*, which served at Southwold for 13 years, was the station's second Atlantic. During her time, she was launched 235 times and saved 70 lives. She was one of only a few Atlantic 21s to have the name on the bow beneath the inflatable sponson. (Nicholas Leach)

ILB house on the Dock Wall

In the late 1980s, the RNLI began a programme to modernise its boathouses. and shore facilities. At Southwold, a new house for the Atlantic was built near the harbour entrance on the Dock Wall opposite the caravan site. The building, designed by architects Mullins Dowse and Partners of Woodbridge, was an L-shape with the main ground floor comprising a changing room and the area in which the boat is housed. A crew room and look-out were located at first floor level. The house was completed by early 1994 and, being larger than the one it replaced, had sufficient space to accommodate the Atlantic 75 since allocated to the station. The marine davit, by which the ILB is launched, can be seen to the left. (Nicholas Leach)

Atlantic 75 *Leslie Tranmer* (B-750), 1999

In 1998 a new Atlantic 75, *Leslie Tranmer*, was sent to Southwold and, unlike previous ILBs, she was fitted with orange sponsons. She was placed on station on 28 October and is seen here on the Dock Wall beneath the launching davit in February 1999 prior to launching. The Atlantic 75, developed from the smaller Atlantic 21, can reach speeds of up to 34 knots. (Nicholas Leach)

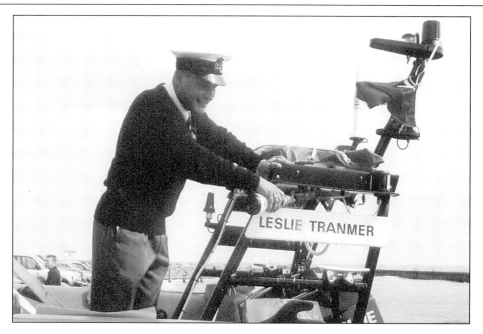

Naming ceremony of Atlantic 75 *Leslie Tranmer* (B-750), 1999

Champagne is poured over the nameplate of Atlantic 75 *Leslie Tranmer* at the end of her naming ceremony on 19 June 1999. Funded by the Annie Tranmer Charitable Trust, she was christened by Mrs Valerie Lewis, daughter of Annie and Leslie Tranmer. (Nicholas Leach)

Atlantic 75 *Leslie Tranmer* (B-750)

Atlantic 75 *Leslie Tranmer* seen leaving the harbour and heading out to sea following her Naming Ceremony on 19 June 1999. The Atlantic 75 was a development of the Atlantic 21 but was slightly larger and faster with improved crew protection. (Nicholas Leach)

Former lifeboat *Alfred Corry* (ON.353)

Alfred Corry has an interesting history and is now back on display in the town. In August 1918, she was sold by the RNLI to Lord Albemarle who had her converted to a yacht named *Alba*, and fitted with an auxiliary engine. After Albemarle sold her, she then had a series of owners and was renamed *Thorfinn*. In 1976 she was bought by John Cragie, the great grandson of her first coxswain, and his family. Under his ownership she was rebuilt, re-rigged, re-engined and her original name was restored. In September 1980 she sailed back to Southwold for the first time in more than 60 years. In the early 1990s John Cragie decided that she should be retired from the sea so she was lifted out of the water. She was donated to a Charitable Trust set up to carry out the restoration work and, on 12 August 1994, was taken by road to Southwold where restoration began. In December 1996, the lifeboat house at the end of Cromer pier was dismantled and purchased by the Trust. In April 1998 it was brought by barge to Southwold and, after considerable repair work had been carried out on the building, *Alfred Corry* was moved into it to be restored and displayed as the centrepiece of a museum about the local lifeboat station. The photograph shows her under sail off Osea Island in the River Blackwater, June 1981 and on display in the old Cromer boathouse. (Top, Richard Barnard; bottom, John Cragie)

Dunwich

Lifeboat House, 1911

The lifeboat station at Dunwich was in operation from 1873 until 1903. This lifeboat house, built in 1873, served throughout the life of the station, housing three different lifeboats. The station was temporarily closed in 1901 due to crew shortages and permanently closed two years later. The small village of Dunwich suffered greatly from erosion by the sea and, at the time this photograph was taken, November 1911, the lifeboat house was at the edge of the beach. The continued undermining inevitably resulted in the collapse of the house, and nothing now remains of this station. (From an old photo in the Jeff Morris Collection)

Thorpeness

Lifeboat house

Between 1853 and 1900, a lifeboat was operated from the village of Thorpeness, approximately two miles north of Aldeburgh. The station was managed by the Aldeburgh local committee, and it was from Aldeburgh that the first lifeboat was transferred. This lifeboat house was built in 1863 and inside in this photograph is probably one of the three self-righting lifeboats named *Ipswich* that served the station between 1862 and 1892, most likely the latter of the three. The third *Ipswich,* a 37ft self-righter pulling 12 oars, served from 1873 to 1892 and is credited with saving 19 lives. The station was closed in 1900 as the area was adequately covered by the two lifeboats at Aldeburgh where a crew could more easily be obtained. (From an old photograph in the author's collection)

Aldeburgh

Freddie Cooper (ON.1193)

Aldeburgh's current lifeboat, 12m Mersey *Freddie Cooper* (ON.1193), driving towards the beach prior to recovery onto her carriage. The introduction in 1993 of *Freddie Cooper,* the station's first 'fast' lifeboat marked the beginning of a new chapter in the history of the station, as described towards the end of this chapter. (From a postcard in the author's collection)

Aldeburgh (ON.304) after capsizing on 7 December 1899

On 7 December 1899, the lifeboat _Aldeburgh_ capsized on service. She had launched through heavy surf to a vessel thought to be aground on the Inner Shoal sandbank. After being struck by two huge waves, she capsized. On board was a crew of 18, of whom 12 were flung overboard and floated ashore. Efforts to right the boat failed and the six trapped beneath drowned. A seventh died three months later from his injuries. This photo shows the upturned lifeboat on the beach. The hole was cut during attempts to release the six trapped men. (RNLI, courtesy of Jeff Morris)

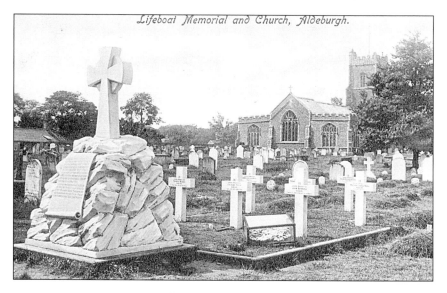

Lifeboat Memorial

The impressive marble statue in the Churchyard was erected in memory of the seven men who gave their lives when the lifeboat _Aldeburgh_ (ON.304) capsized on 7 December 1899. The memorial stands at the head of the graves of those who were lost. When the lifeboat capsized, one of the crew who had been washed ashore, Charles Ward, went back into the surf to try to help the men trapped inside. For his courage and determination, the RNLI awarded him the Silver medal. (From an old postcard supplied by Paul Russell)

Bolton (ON.352), 1901-02

The Kessingland No.1 lifeboat *Bolton* was the second of two lifeboats that served at Aldeburgh following the capsizing of *Aldeburgh*. A 43ft Norfolk & Suffolk, *Bolton* had been built in 1893 for Kessingland and was temporarily moved to Aldeburgh in 1901 to replace *Reserve No.1* (ON.270), the lifeboat sent immediately after the 1899 capsize. While at Aldeburgh, *Bolton* was launched on service once, on 27 February 1902, when she saved the crew of the barque *Loveid,* of Portsgrund. (From an old photo loaned by Ken Brown, by courtesy of Jeff Morris)

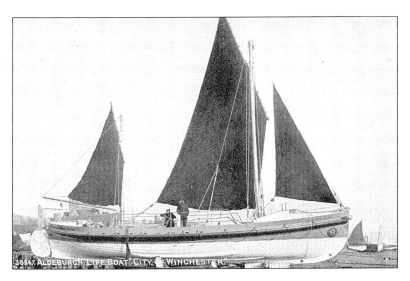

City of Winchester (ON.482), 1902-28

After the lifeboat disaster of 1899, a large 46ft sailing lifeboat was built for Aldeburgh by Thames Iron Works at Blackwall, equipped with 12 oars. Funded by the Winchester Lifeboat Fund, *City of Winchester* was launched on service 43 times and saved 40 lives while at Aldeburgh. She is seen here on the beach with her sails up, presumably for the benefit of the photographer from the Photochrom Company Ltd, London. (From an old postcard supplied by David Gooch)

Launching *City of Winchester* (ON.482)

Launching a lifeboat as large as *City of Winchester* required a considerable effort on the part of the launchers. A haul-off warp laid off the beach helped, and the crew can be seen pulling on it to get the lifeboat through the surf and away. (From an old postcard supplied by Paul Russell)

Launching *City of Winchester* (ON.482)

This dramatic photo shows *City of Winchester* being launched off the beach with the mizzen sail set to steady the lifeboat, and launchers using a pushing pole. As this photo illustrates, launching the heavy lifeboat into breaking surf was a difficult task. Often several hours and considerable energy would be expended just to get the lifeboat afloat. (Roger Wiltshire)

Edward Z Dresden (ON.545), 1905-29

In 1905, a No.2 station was opened after the neighbouring stations at Thorpeness and Dunwich had been closed in 1900 and 1903 respectively. The Liverpool lifeboat *Edward Z Dresden* was sent to Aldeburgh where, with crew available, operating a second lifeboat was a viable way to maintain coverage of this coast. She was provided out of the legacy of Edmond Dresden, of London, and named after his father. (From an old postcard supplied by a Shoreline member)

Launching *Edward Z Dresden* (ON.545)

Although most of the pulling lifeboats in Suffolk were of the Norfolk & Suffolk type, at some stations a Liverpool type boat was used. *Edward Z Dresden*, the No.2 lifeboat from 1905 until 1929, was a 35ft by 10ft 9in Liverpool type. This photograph, with the sea flat calm, shows the boat with her mainsail raised and mizzen being raised. This sail plan was almost identical to that of the Norfolk & Suffolk type widely used throughout East Anglia. (Roger Wiltshire)

Coxswain James Cable

James Cable became Coxswain in January 1888 and was three times awarded the RNLI's Silver medal. He retired at the end of August 1917 after half a century of service in the crew. As well as the RNLI medals, he also received the Norwegian Silver Medal and the Royal Humane Society Medal for Life-saving. He had also received a silver box from the Mayor and Corporation of Aldeburgh for going out in his own boat and rescuing four men. He was succeeded as coxswain by Charles Mann, but remains one of the best known of all Aldeburgh coxswains. (RNLI Postcard)

Edward Z Dresden (ON.545) on parade

Dated April 1909, this photograph shows the No.2 lifeboat *Edward Z Dresden* being hauled through the streets of Aldeburgh, almost certainly for publicity purposes. The carriage enabled the lifeboat to be paraded through the town whose inhabitants were clearly proud of their lifeboat. In the lifeboat's stern, the Coxswain, James Cable (with the beard), can be seen. (From an old postcard supplied by Roger Wiltshire)

City of Winchester (ON.482) and *Edward Z Dresden* (ON.545)

The beach at Aldeburgh with, on the left No.2 lifeboat *Edward Z Dresden,* on the right No.1 lifeboat *City of Winchester,* and the North Lookout Tower in the background. Both lifeboats were kept in the open as, somewhat unusually, no lifeboat house was built. *Edward Z Dresden* is on a launching carriage, although in later years she was launched across the beach over skids. (From an old postcard supplied by David Gooch)

Motor lifeboat *William MacPherson* (ON.620) on trials, 1930

In 1930, the 1912-built 43ft Watson motor lifeboat *William MacPherson* was sent to Aldeburgh for launching trials off the beach. The lifeboat, stationed at Campbeltown from 1912 until 1929, arrived on 10 February 1930 and was used for a series of trials to prove the viability of operating a motor lifeboat from the beach. The success of these trials resulted in a new motor lifeboat being built specifically for the station. *William MacPherson* was subsequently transferred to Pwllheli, where she served until 1940. (From an old postcard supplied by David Gooch)

Abdy Beauclerk (ON.751), 1931-59

Aldeburgh's first motor lifeboat, 41ft Beach *Abdy Beauclerk,* on her launching cradle on the beach. This type of lifeboat was based on the 41ft Watson design but had greater breadth and a broad, heavy iron keel so it would withstand the rigours of beach launching. The propellers were housed in tunnels, which can clearly be seen, and auxiliary sails were carried. In this postcard, a small group has just been shown over the boat. (From an old postcard supplied by David Gooch)

Abdy Beauclerk
(ON.751)
1931-59

In 1931 Aldeburgh received its first motor lifeboat, the 41ft Beach type *Abdy Beauclerk,* built by J S White. The new lifeboat was funded from the legacy of Mrs Jane Elizabeth King, of St Leonards-on-Sea, and was named on 27 May 1932 by Prince George. During her 28 years of service at Aldeburgh, she saved 141 lives and launched 125 times on service. (From an old postcard supplied by Roger Wiltshire)

The Lifeboat, Aldeburgh

Abdy Beauclerk (ON.751) on the beach

This fine photograph of *Abdy Beauclerk* was taken during her early years on station. The cradle and wooden slip over the beach have yet to be constructed. This lifeboat's most notable rescue was undertaken on 23 November 1938 when she saved a total of four people from the Rochester barges *Grecian* and *Astrild*. The lifeboat was taken through heavy seas in gale force winds to successfully complete the rescue, for which the Bronze medal was awarded to Coxswain George Chatten for outstanding seamanship. (From an old postcard supplied by a Shoreline member)

No.2 lifeboat *Lucy Lavers* (ON.832), 1957

The last No.2 lifeboat to serve at Aldeburgh was the 35ft 6in Liverpool motor lifeboat *Lucy Lavers,* built in 1940 at the Cowes yard of Groves & Guttridge. She was one of only a handful of lifeboats to be completed during World War II. She served at Aldeburgh until February 1959, and is credited with saving seven lives during almost two decades of service. She is seen at sea on 10 August 1957 during the station's annual Flag Day, with a steadying sail set as she heads to sea. (Jeff Morris)

Abdy Beauclerk (ON.751) and Lucy Lavers (ON.832), 1957

This interesting view overlooking the shingle beach at Aldeburgh, with the Crag Path to the left running parallel to the shore, shows the station's two lifeboats at the heads of their respective slipways. Nearest camera is the 35ft 6in Liverpool *Lucy Lavers,* the No.2 boat, with the 41ft Beach *Abdy Beauclerk* behind. In the background, further down the beach, can be seen Aldeburgh's famous Moot Hall. (From an old postcard supplied by Paul Russell)

Abdy Beauclerk (ON.751) and Lucy Lavers (ON.832), 1958

Between 1905 and 1959, two lifeboats were operated at Aldeburgh, known as No.1 and No.2 lifeboats. This photograph shows the two boats on station in July 1958. Both were kept on launching cradles at the head of the shingle beach and launched down the wooden slipway built part of the way to the sea. On the left is *Lucy Lavers,* No.2 lifeboat from 1940 to 1959, and on the right *Abdy Beauclerk,* the No.1 lifeboat. (Jeff Morris)

Abdy Beauclerk (ON.751), Lifeboat Day, 1958

The 41ft Beach lifeboat *Abdy Beauclerk,* built in 1931, served at Aldeburgh from December 1931 until February 1959. She is seen here in August 1958 returning to the beach at Aldeburgh after a demonstration launch for the station's annual Flag Day. (Jeff Morris)

Naming ceremony of *The Alfred and Patience Gottwald* (ON.946), 1959

In February 1959 a new 42ft Beach lifeboat, *The Alfred and Patience Gottwald,* was sent to Aldeburgh. Built by J S White at East Cowes, she was funded from the legacy of Mrs Patience Gottwald, of Southport. She was named at a ceremony on 15 July 1959 by the Countess of Cairns. This photograph shows the bottle of champagne breaking over the bow of the new lifeboat at the end of the naming ceremony. (From an old postcard supplied by David Gooch)

The Alfred and Patience Gottwald (ON.946), 1959-79

The Alfred and Patience Gottwald, completed in 1959, was one of the last Beach class boats to be built. The Beach lifeboats were specially designed for being launched over a beach, an operation which placed extra stresses and strains on their hulls. *The Alfred and Patience Gottwald* was 42ft in length and 12ft 3in in breadth, more than 6in broader than the standard 42ft Watson upon which the design was based. She had a mizzen mast at the stern on which a steadying sail could be mounted. During her two decades at Aldeburgh, she saved 21 lives. (J W Markham)

Service launch of *The Alfred and Patience Gottwald* (ON.946), 1965

Launching at 6.45am on 1 September 1965, *The Alfred and Patience Gottwald* puts out to the Dutch coaster *Texel*, which was sinking 32 miles east of Aldeburgh. The coaster's crew were picked up by a steamer, so the lifeboat was recalled. (Jeff Morris)

Two lifeboats on the beach, 1966

Reserve 41ft Beach lifeboat *Charles Cooper Henderson* (ON.761) on the right, with Aldeburgh's own lifeboat *The Alfred and Patience Gottwald* (ON.946) on the left. This photograph was taken on 2 July 1966, the day after the reserve lifeboat had arrived for temporary duty as Aldeburgh's own lifeboat went for a routine overhaul. The cradle and turntable on which the lifeboats were kept, built at the head of the beach during the 1950s, can clearly be seen. (Jeff Morris)

Reserve lifeboat *Charles Cooper Henderson* (ON.761)

The 41ft Beach lifeboat *Charles Cooper Henderson,* built in 1933, was stationed at Dungeness for until 1957. She was then placed in the Reserve fleet and served as a Reserve lifeboat at Aldeburgh on three different occasions, in 1966, 1968 and 1973-4. In January 1976 she was sold by the RNLI and, in private ownership, was converted into the yacht *Caresana.* (J W Markham)

Arrival of *James Cable* (ON.1068), 1982

The new 37ft 6in Rother lifeboat *James Cable* beaching at Aldeburgh on 8 June 1982. She served at Aldeburgh for just over a decade, and was the last 37ft 6in Rother class to be built by the RNLI. As she approaches the beach, the lifeboatman on the bow is ready to throw a line to the shore helpers to enable the winch cable to be attached to the lifeboat and haul the boat out of the water to the top of the slipway ready for launching again. (Jeff Morris)

James Cable (ON.1068), 1982-93

James Cable launching on exercise on 8 June 1982, the day after she arrived on station. After gaining speed down the slipway built across the top part of the beach, the lifeboat's momentum would carry her across the shingle and into the sea. *James Cable* served from June 1982 until November 1993, and was launched 54 times on service and saved 24 lives. (Jeff Morris)

Naming ceremony of *James Cable* (ON.1068), 1982

Lifeboat crew and station officials during the naming ceremony of *James Cable* on 20 September 1982. Built by William Osborne, at Littlehampton, she was funded by the Aldeburgh Lifeboat Appeal and named in memory of one of Aldeburgh's most famous coxswains. (Jeff Morris)

Naming ceremony of *James Cable* (ON.1068), 1982

At the end of the formal ceremony on 20 September 1982, *James Cable* is launched for a demonstration with HRH The Duke of Kent on board. in this dramatic photograph of the boat entering the water, the tunnels at the stern of the lifeboat, which protect the twin propellers, can clearly be seen. (Jeff Morris)

Naming ceremony of *James Cable* (ON.1068), 1982

Following her naming ceremony on 20 September 1982, *James Cable* put to sea with HRH The Duke of Kent on board. Having just named the lifeboat, the Duke can be seen on board, second from left, as the lifeboat passes the beach where crowds of well-wishers and supporters had assembled for the occasion. (Jeff Morris)

Inshore lifeboat D-270, 1980-88

An inshore lfieboat was stationed at Aldeburgh in 1977 to supplement the all-weather lifeboat. In March 1980, Great Yarmouth Round Table funded a new ILB for the station, D-270, which served for eight years. This ILB, seen in July 1984 outside the North Lookout in which she was housed, was launched from a standard trolley across the beach. (Jeff Morris)

Relief lifeboat *Charles Dibdin (Civil Service No.32)* (ON.948), 1987

Built in 1959, the 42ft Beach lifeboat *Charles Dibdin (Civil Service No.32)* served at Walmer and Eastbourne before being placed on station at Aldeburgh in August 1979. She stayed until June 1982, after which she was placed in the Relief Fleet. She is seen here on 31 March 1987 on relief duty in place of the 37ft 6in Rother *James Cable* which was undergoing overhaul. (Paul Russell)

James Cable (ON.1068), 1990

Not only was 37ft 6in Rother *James Cable* the last beach launched lifeboat at Aldeburgh, but also the last displacement-hulled lifeboat at any of the RNLI's stations. Seen here on the launching cradle at the head of the slipway, she was a familiar sight on Aldeburgh's beach for more than a decade. The cradle, clearly visible in this photograph taken in August 1990, was mounted on a turntable so the boat could be recovered bow first up the beach, turned through 180 degrees to face the sea and be ready for service again. (Nicholas Leach)

Launching trials, May 1990

In May 1990, trials were held to assess whether launching the lifeboat from a carriage, a practice used at many lifeboat stations, was possible across Aldeburgh's shingle beach. The trials, which took place on 23 May 1990, involved relief 12m Mersey *Lifeboat Care* (ON.1148) and Talus MB-H tractor T91. Their success resulted in the allocation of a Mersey lifeboat to the station as the RNLI pursued a policy of replacing the 9-knot displacement hulled lifeboats, such as the 37ft 6in Rother, with 'fast' lifeboats capable of speeds of 15 knots or more. (Paul Russell)

James Cable (ON.1068) and *Lifetime Care* (ON.1148), May 1990

Relief 12m Mersey *Lifeboat Care* on her launching carriage, with the station's own lifeboat, 37ft 6in Rother *James Cable,* on the cradle at the head of the slipway. In this photograph, the different hull shapes of the two lifeboats can be seen. The Mersey's semi-planing hull gives the boat a speed of 16 knots, almost twice that of the Rother. (Paul Russell)

Arrival of *Freddie Cooper* (ON.1193), November 1993

On 30 November 1993, 12m Mersey *Freddie Cooper* arrived on station (after passage from Harwich) to replace *James Cable*. It was a notable day for the station, and the new lifeboat was greeted by a large crowd including the RNLI's Director, Lieut Commander Brian Miles. With her arrival on station, the RNLI had completed the upgrading of its fleet of lifeboats so that all were capable of speeds of 14 knots or more. She is seen here being hauled up the beach for the first time. (Nicholas Leach)

Naming ceremony of *Freddie Cooper* (ON.1193), May 1994

12m Mersey *Freddie Cooper* seen on her carriage after her naming ceremony on 31 May 1994. She was funded from the legacy of Mrs Winifred May Cooper in memory of a former director of East Midland Allied Press Ltd and named by HRH The Duke of Kent. (Paul Russell)

Penza Lifeboat house

In order to house the new carriage-launched lifeboat, a lifeboat house was built on the beach on the site occupied hitherto by the turntable and launchways. The building consisted of two houses adjacent to each other, for lifeboat and launching tractor, linked by a single-storey section. The new building was one of eight funded from the legacy of Mrs Eugenie Boucher. All are known as 'Penza' lifeboat houses after the town in south-east Russia, approximately 350 miles from Moscow, which was the home of Mrs Boucher until the 1920s. (Nicholas Leach)

North Lookout ILB house

A year after the ILB entered service at Aldeburgh, the Old North Lookout on the promenade, used by the Fishermen's Guild, was adapted to house the station's D class inflatable. The building was extended in 1997 so that the bladed tractor, used for flattening the shingle to ease the launch of the all-weather lifeboat, could be accommodated. This lookout on the beach originally served as the headquarters of the North Company of beachmen in the 19th century. (Nicholas Leach)

Rescue of yacht *Red House Lugger*, 29 August 1996

This dramatic photograph, taken from the Lowestoft lifeboat *Spirit of Lowestoft*, shows *Freddie Cooper* during the service to the yacht *Red House Lugger*. In winds gusting to force 11, the ferry *Norking* provided some shelter as *Freddie Cooper* saved three from the yacht, while three others were rescued by the Lowestoft lifeboat, which also towed the yacht to safety. For this service, Coxswain Ian Firman was awarded the Bronze medal. (Aldeburgh Lifeboat Station)

D class inflatable *Bob Savage* (D-520), 1997

D class inflatable *Bob Savage* was placed on station in June 1997. Funded from the gift of Mr and Mrs Hugh Turner, she was named at a ceremony on 23 August 1997 after a former senior helmsman of the ILB who was drowned in August 1990 whilst on passage in a yacht from the Baltic. (Photo by courtesy of Aldeburgh Lifeboat Station)

Recovery of 12m Mersey *Freddie Cooper* (ON.1193), 2000

Freddie Cooper returning from refit at West Custom Marine, Lymington, on 27 October 2000. In the top photo, the shore helpers are attaching the tractor's winch wire preparing to pull her out of the water after she has been beached. In the bottom photo, the lifeboat has been recovered onto the launching carriage. (Peter Edey)

Bury St Edmunds

Self-righting lifeboat on display

During the late 19th century, activities to raise funds for the Royal National Lifeboat Institution became commonplace in towns and cities throughout Britain as the Institution appealed to the public for donations. Lifeboat Saturday, introduced in the 1890s, became a common event at which to raise funds for the RNLI. This postcard depicts a standard self-righting lifeboat on her carriage in Bury St Edmunds prior to the lifeboat being paraded through the town. Her crew, in their cork life-jackets, lend an authenticity to the proceedings in a town that is almost as far inland as it is possible to get in Suffolk. (Roger Wiltshire)

Appendices

A. Lifeboat stations in Suffolk, from north to south

Station	Opened	RNLI	Closed	Motor	Inshore
Corton	1869	1869	1879		
Lowestoft	1801		1805		
	1807	1855		1921	
No.2	1870	1870	1912		
Oulton Broad	2001	2001			2001
Pakefield	1840	1855	1922		
No.2	1871	1871	1895		
Kessingland	1867	1867	1936		
At Benacre	1870	1870	1918		
No.3	1884	1884	1896		
Southwold	1841	1854	1940	1925	1963
No.2	1866	1866	1920		
Dunwich	1873	1873	1903		
Sizewell	1826	1826*	1851		
Thorpeness	1853	1855	1900		
No.2	1860	1860	1863		
Aldeburgh	1851	1855		1930	1977
No.2	1905	1905	1959	1940	
Orford	1826	1826*	1835		
Hollesley Bay	1801		1825		
Woodbridge Haven	1825	1825*	1853		

*Operated by the Suffolk Association of the Royal National Institution for the Preservation of Life from Shipwreck, the forerunner of the RNLI

B. Bibliography and further reading

Cable, James (nd): *A Lifeboatman's Days* (John Lovett, Aldeburgh).

Cooper, Ernest Read (1912): *Seventy Years of the Southwold Life-boats* (Southwold Press, Southwold).

— (1937): *Storm Warriors of the Suffolk Coast* (Heath Cranton).

Leach, Nicholas (1992): *The Origins of the Lifeboat Service*.

— (1998): *Lifeboat Stations of East Anglia: An Illustrated Guide* (Norfolk & Suffolk Research Group, Cheddington, Beds).

— (1999): *For Those In Peril: The Lifeboat Service of the United Kingdom and Republic of Station, station by station* (Silver Link Publishing Ltd, Peterborough).

Malster, Robert (1969): 'Suffolk Lifeboats - The First Quarter Century', in *Mariners Mirror*, Vol.55, pp.263-280.

— (1974): *Saved from the Sea: The story of life-saving services on the East Anglian coast* (Terence Dalton, Lavenham, Suffolk).

— (1982): *Lowestoft: East Coast Port* (Terence Dalton, Lavenham, Suffolk).

Mitchley, Jack (1973): *The Story of Lowestoft Lifeboats, Part 1 1801-1876* (Port of Lowestoft Research Society).

Mitchley, Jack; Jones, Stuart; and Keith, William (1996): *The Story of Lowestoft Lifeboats, Part 2 1877-1924* (Port of Lowestoft Research Society).

Morris, Jeff (1994): *The Story of the Aldeburgh Lifeboats*.

Wiltshire, Roger (1994): *Norfolk's Lifeboats: A Portrait in Photographs and Picture Postcards* (S B Publications, Seaford, Sussex).